At School
Telling Time by the Half Hour

by Alice Proctor

WEEKLY READER®
PUBLISHING

Math and Curriculum Consultant:
Debra Voege, M.A.,
Science and Math Curriculum Resource Teacher

Please visit our web site at: www.garethstevens.com
For a free color catalog describing our list of high-quality books,
call 1-800-542-2595 (USA) or 1-800-387-3178 (Canada).

Library of Congress Cataloging-in-Publication Data

Proctor, Alice, 1967-
    At school: telling time by the half hour / Alice Proctor.
       p. cm. — (I can tell time)
    ISBN-10: 0-8368-8390-X — ISBN-13: 978-0-8368-8390-9 (lib. bdg.)
    ISBN-10: 0-8368-8395-0 — ISBN-13: 978-0-8368-8395-4 (softcover)
    1. Time—Juvenile literature. 2. Schools—Juvenile literature. I. Title.
QB209.5.P759   2007
529'.7—dc22   2007017438

This North American edition first published in 2008 by
Weekly Reader® Books
An imprint of Gareth Stevens Publishing
1 Reader's Digest Road
Pleasantville, NY 10570-7000 USA

This U.S. edition copyright © 2008 by Gareth Stevens, Inc. Original edition
copyright © 2007 by ticktock Entertainment Ltd. First published in Great Britain
in 2007 by ticktock Media Ltd., Unit 2, Orchard Business Centre, North Farm Road,
Tunbridge Wells, Kent, TN2 3XF, United Kingdom.

Gareth Stevens series editor: Dorothy L. Gibbs
Gareth Stevens graphic design and cover design: Dave Kowalski
Gareth Stevens art direction: Tammy West

Picture credits: (t=top, b=bottom, c=center, l=left, r=right)
Alamy: (Image Source Black) 19t, 23tl, (Stockbyte Silver) cover. Banana Stock: 13t, 22tl.
Corbis: 9t, 19b, 23tr. Getty: 18. Reflexstock: 17t. Shutterstock: 9b, 12 all, 13b, 15, 20 both,
21 both, 22tr, 22tcl, 22cr, 23tc, 23c, 23bl, 23br. Superstock: 1, 4l, 8l, 10, 11 both, 14, 16,
17b, 22bcl, 23tcl. Ticktock Media Archive: 4r, 5 both, 6, 7 both, 8r, 22bc, 23bcl, 24 both.

Every effort has been made to trace the copyright holders for the pictures used in this book.
We apologize in advance for any unintentional omissions and would be pleased to insert the
appropriate acknowledgements in any subsequent edition.

Printed in the United States of America

1 2 3 4 5 6 7 8 9 11 10 09 08 07

Contents

Glossary words are printed in **boldface** type in the text.

Half Past

Not all lessons at school start at an exact hour. Let's learn what time it is when the big hand is pointing at the 6.

Half Past 10

Look at the big hand on this watch. It is pointing at the 6.

Now look at the little hand. It has moved past the 10. It is halfway between 10 and 11.

The time on this watch is **half past** 10.

We say "half past" because the big hand has moved halfway around the face of the clock.

Half Past 5

On this clock, the little hand has moved past the 5. It is halfway between 5 and 6. The big hand pointing at the 6 tells us the time is half past 5.

Digital Clocks

Digital clocks do not have hands. Instead, two numbers show the time. The first number shows the hour. The second number shows the number of minutes past the hour.

When a digital clock shows 30 minutes past the hour, the time is half past. On this digital watch, the time is half past 7.

Instead of half past 7, we can also say seven-thirty.

My Day at School

Monday is finally here. I can't wait to get to school and see all my friends again.

Time to Get Up

7 o'clock

The alarm clock rings at 7 o'clock in the **morning**. I get up right away. First, I eat breakfast. Today, I am having fresh fruit and juice. I love to eat fruit!

Getting Ready for School

Half past 7

After breakfast,
I brush my teeth.
Then I get dressed.

8 o'clock

Mom walks
with me to
the bus
stop. On the
way, we meet my
friend Emma. Hurry, Emma!
I see the school bus coming!

Going to the Bus

What time do you leave for school in the morning?

9

My Morning Lesson

When we get to school, Emma and I go to our classroom. Our teacher is there waiting for us.

Time to Learn

9 o'clock

When the bell rings at 9 o'clock, we are all sitting at our desks. Our teacher calls our names to see who is here.

Then it is time to start our lessons. Math is our first lesson today. We are learning how to add and subtract numbers.

Computer Math

10 o'clock

We get to practice our math on the computer for 30 minutes.

Playtime

Half past 10

Hooray! It's time for recess. The Sun is shining. We can play outside today!

How long is recess time at your school?

Science and Lunch

Recess lasts for half an hour. Now it is time for our science lesson.

Creepy Crawlers

11 o'clock
Our teacher tells us all about small creatures that live outdoors.

Spiders have eight legs.

Ladybugs have six legs.

Worms have no legs at all!

Outdoor Science

Half past 11

Half an hour later, we go
outside to look for spiders,
insects, and worms. I find a huge
black spider! My teacher puts it in a jar so
we can look at it closely. Then we let it go.

We wash our hands when we come back inside. It is time for lunch!

Pasta Surprise!

12 o'clock

Emma and I eat
spaghetti for
lunch. It
reminds us
of the worms we
saw outside. Yuck!

What time do you eat lunch at school?

Afternoon Lessons

After lunch, we are ready for more lessons. This afternoon, we have English and art.

Reading and Writing

1 o'clock

For our reading lesson today, we go to the school library. I can choose any book I want to read. I pick a book about planets.

Next, we all write a story. Our teacher says to give the story a surprise ending. I write about a trip to the planet Mars.

Art Class

2 o'clock

It is painting day in art class. I paint a picture of me and my dad at the park.

What is your favorite class at school?

The School Day Ends

School is almost over. For the last half hour of the day, we have a spelling lesson.

Time to Spell

3 o'clock

Our teacher puts some new spelling words on the blackboard. I practice them with my friend Joanna.

family   castle
vacation   laugh
train   straw
ocean   knock

Time to Go Home

Half past 3

School is over now. My Dad is waiting outside to take me home. He has been shopping! I wonder if he has a surprise for me!

Game Time

4 o'clock

My dad bought me a badminton set! We have time to play a few games before dinner.

What time does your school day end?

Time at Home

Mom gets home from work at 5 o'clock. I show her my new badminton set. I also tell her about the big, black spider I found at school.

Dinnertime

Half past 5

While mom makes dinner, I do my homework.

At dinner, we make plans for next **weekend**. We are going camping!

Story Time

6 o'clock

After dinner, I read a book to my little sister. I am helping her learn the alphabet.

Then I take a bath and get ready for bed.

Bedtime

Half past 7

I had a great day at school. Now I am very tired.

What time do you go to bed?

Time Facts

Clocks and watches measure time. Here are some special kinds of clocks and watches. How many of them have you seen before?

Hourglass
An hourglass uses sand to measure time. The sand takes a certain amount of time to flow from the top of the hourglass to the bottom.

Sundial
A sundial has a face like a clock. As the Sun moves across the sky, a flat pointer in the center of the sundial makes a shadow. The shadow points to the time as it moves around the sundial.

Pocket Watch

This kind of watch got its name from its size. It is small enough to fit into a pocket. The first pocket watch was made about four hundred years ago.

Grandfather Clock

This tall clock has a long **pendulum** that swings from side to side at a steady pace. The swinging pendulum turns gears inside the clock. The gears move the clock's hands.

What other types of clocks have you seen?

Times to Remember

Play this fun time game with a friend.

Each player needs a small object, or counter, to move around the board. You also need a die. (A die is one cube in a pair of dice.) Take turns throwing the die to see how many spaces to move. Follow the numbered squares to move around the board. If you land on a star, follow the trail of stars up the board. If you land on a sad face, follow the arrow down the board. Tell the time on the clocks as you go along!

do homework
33

34

dinner
35

forgot your school bag
32

31

30

spill some paint
19

17

18

recess time
16

15

14

start here
1

alarm rings
2

3

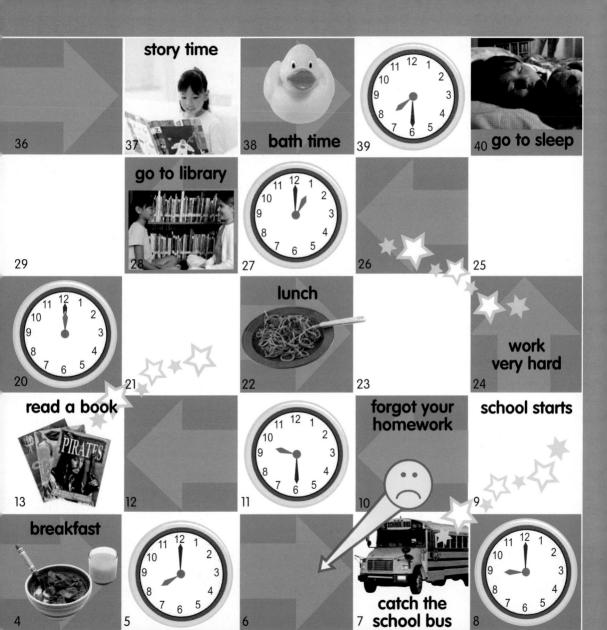

Glossary

afternoon – the part of a day between 12 o'clock noon and the time when the Sun starts to set

day – a period of time that starts and ends at 12 o'clock midnight and lasts 24 hours

half an hour – 30 minutes, or half of the 60 minutes in 1 hour

half past – any time when the big hand on a clock is pointing exactly at the 6, showing that half an hour has passed

hour – a measure of time that equals 60 minutes. Each day has 24 hours.

minute – a measure of time that equals 60 seconds. Each hour has 60 minutes.

morning – the part of a day between 12 o'clock midnight and 12 o'clock noon

o'clock – any hour of the day when the big hand on a clock is pointing exactly at the 12. The little hand shows what hour it is.

pendulum – a weight that hangs on a chain inside a clock and swings back and forth with a steady movement to measure time. The movement of the pendulum turns gears in the clock. The gears move the clock's hands to show the time.

week – a measure of time that equals 7 days

weekend – the two days at the end of a week, which are Saturday and Sunday

Answers

The time is exactly 10 o'clock.

The little hand is pointing at the 8. The big hand is pointing at the 12. The time is exactly 8 o'clock.